A
C
B
AF579420

To my father, whose passion for knowledge fueled my own. This book is a grateful nod to the curiosity you cultivated in me.

This Book Belongs too:

Once upon a time in a lively orchard, there was a special apple named Newton. Newton wasn't an ordinary apple; he was a curious and talkative one who loved to share the wonders of physics with his young friends.

Legend has it, that Newton was the apple that fell on Sir Isaac Newton's head! Sir Isaac Newton was a brilliant scientist who lived a long time ago. He was like a superhero for science!

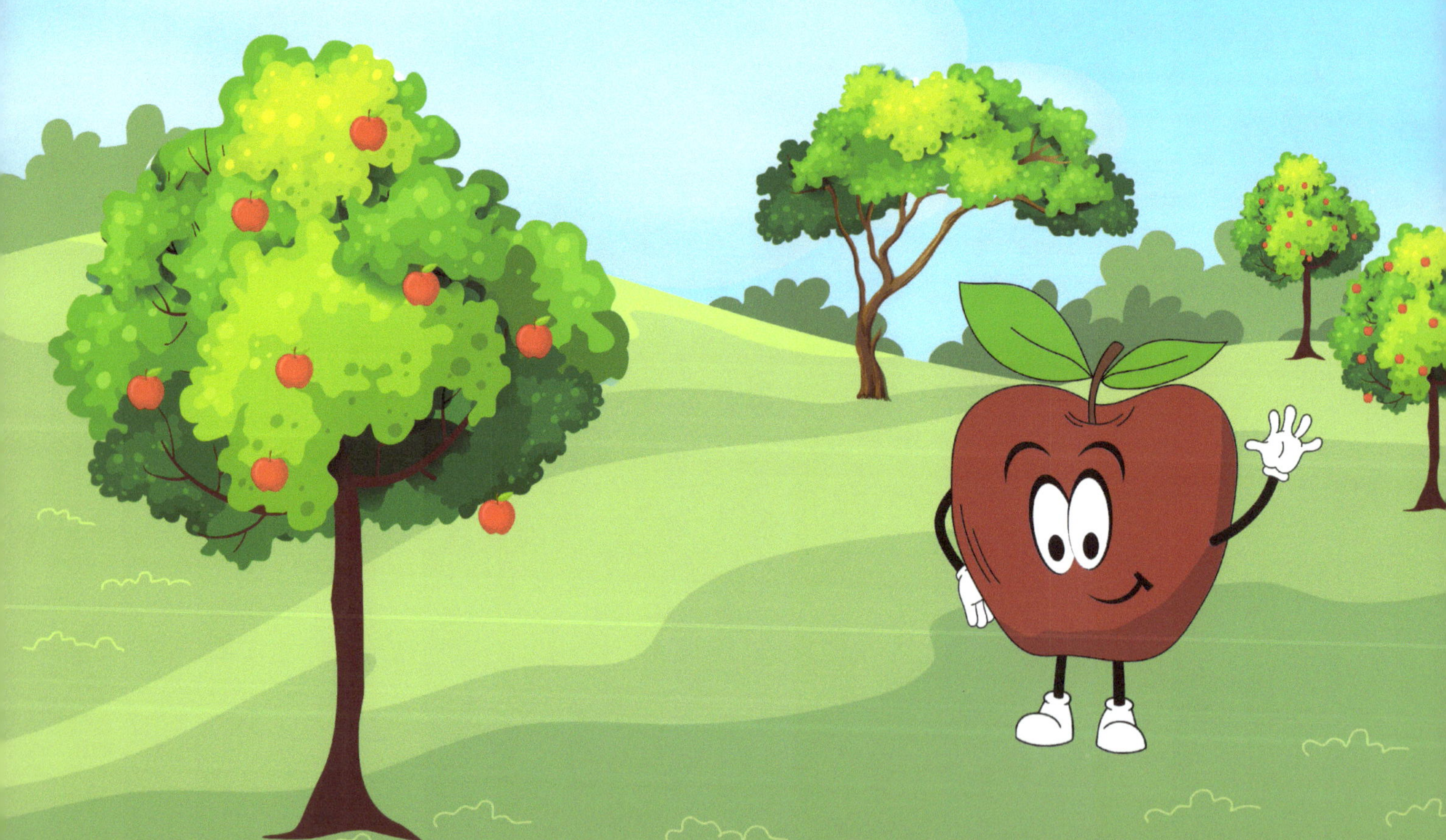

Physics helps us understand how things work in the world around us. It explores the secrets of motion, why objects fall, how things bounce, and even why a swing moves back and forth. So, when we learn physics, we're like detectives unlocking the mysteries of how everything in our playful world moves and interacts!

GRAVITY

One sunny morning, as the apple orchard came alive with laughter, Newton gathered a group of little apples. Their eyes sparkled with curiosity as Newton welcomed them, "Hello, my delightful friends! Today, I'm going to take you on an enchanting journey through the magical world of physics!"

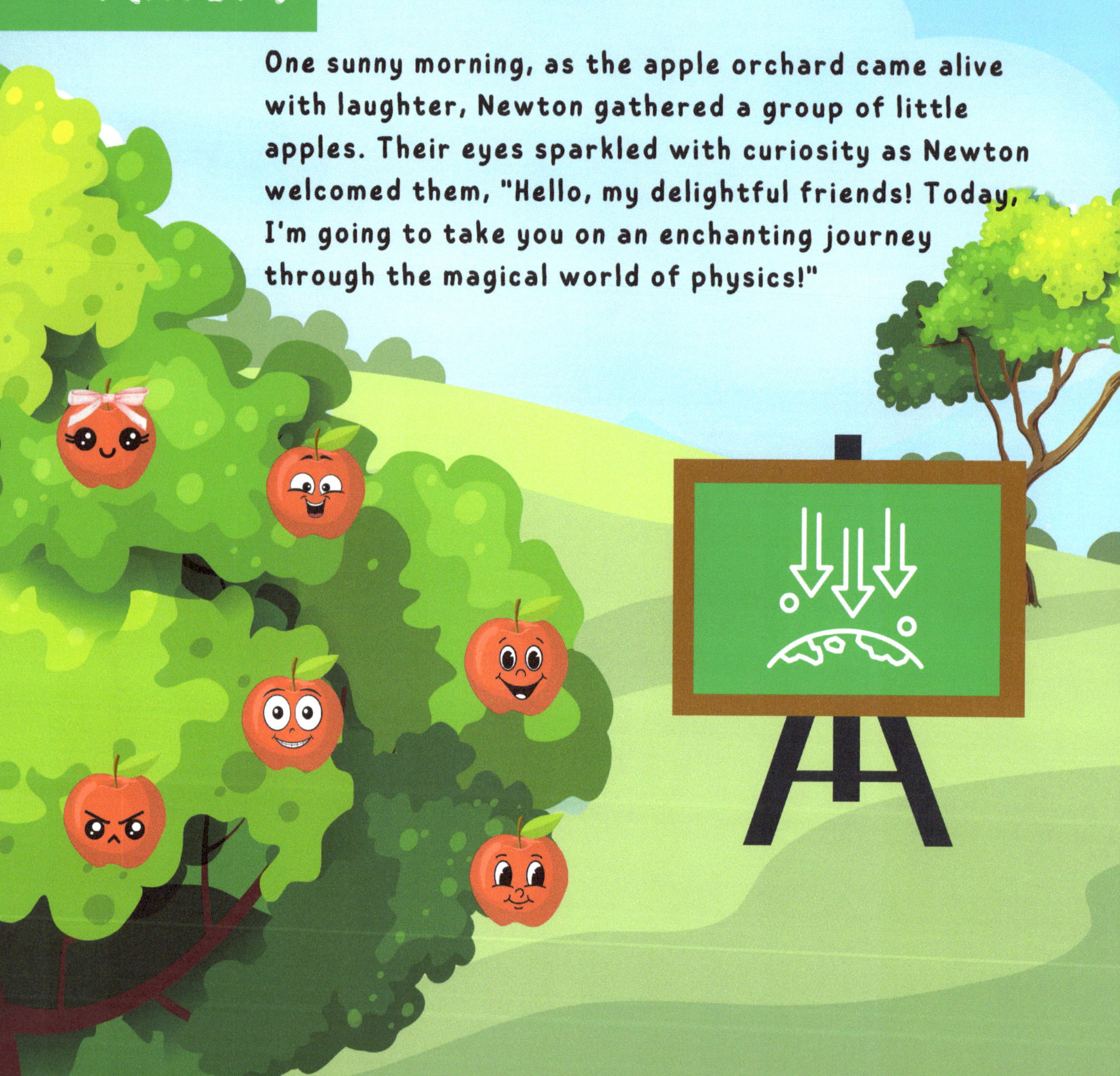

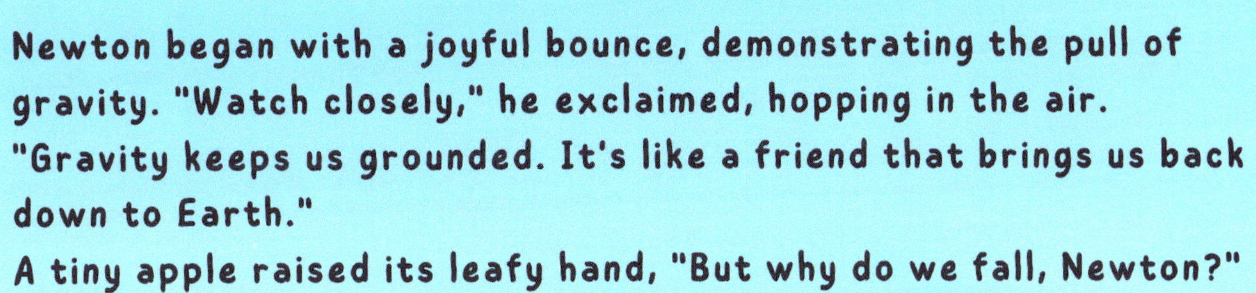

Newton began with a joyful bounce, demonstrating the pull of gravity. "Watch closely," he exclaimed, hopping in the air. "Gravity keeps us grounded. It's like a friend that brings us back down to Earth."

A tiny apple raised its leafy hand, "But why do we fall, Newton?" Newton chuckled and replied, "Ah, excellent question! **Gravity** is what pulls us toward the center of the Earth. It's what makes everything, even us apples, stick to the ground."

POTENTIAL ENERGY

Newton, our orchard physicist, loves swings because they're full of interesting forces! When you pull a swing back and let it go, you're giving it potential energy. As the swing starts moving, potential energy turns into kinetic energy – the energy of motion.

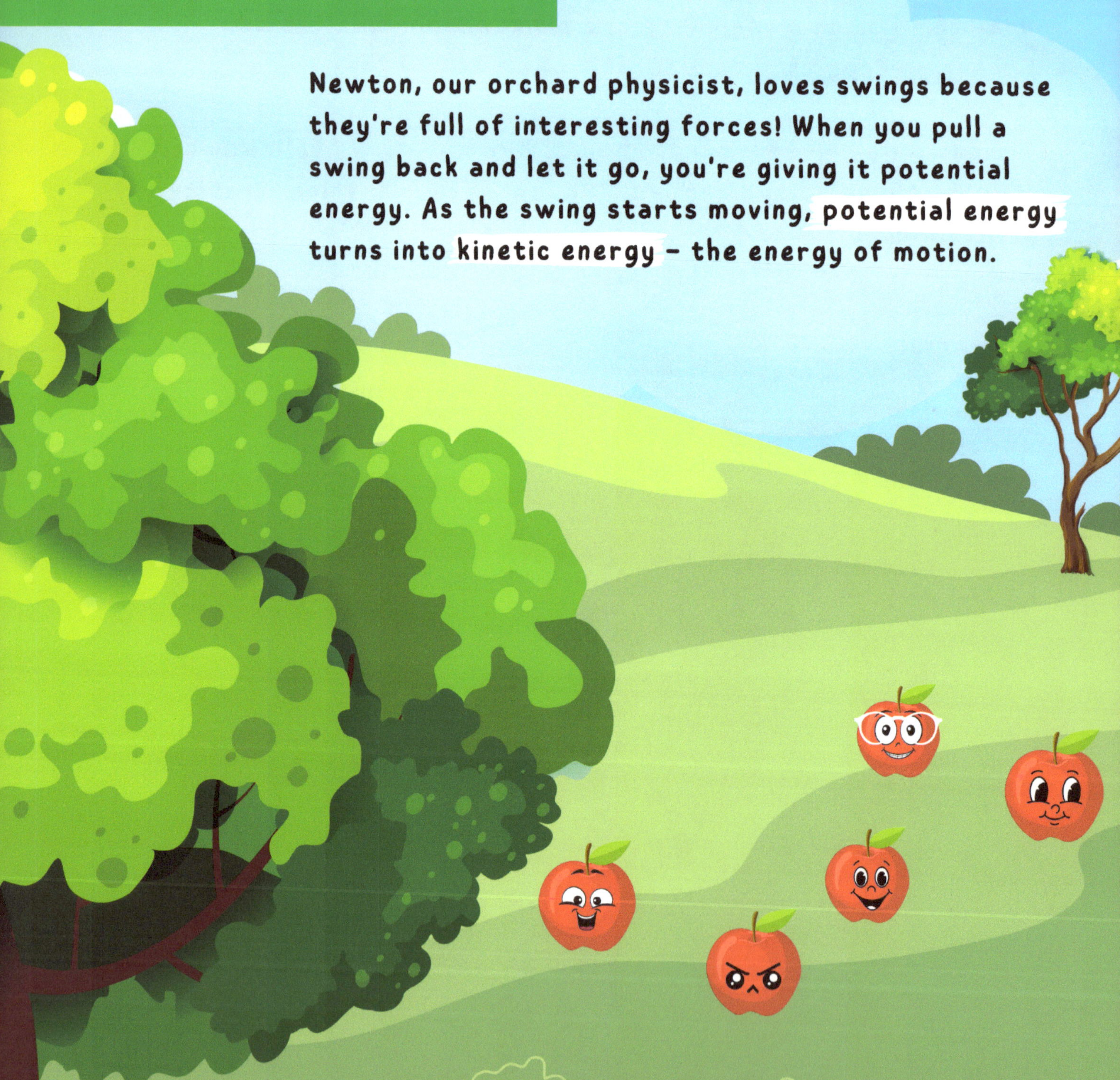

KINETIC ENERGY

But, as you swing higher, you use up some of that energy fighting against air resistance and friction from the chains. Over time, your swing slows down. It's all part of the forces at play in our orchard swing.

INERTIA

Newton, our inquisitive apple friend, loves to teach about the magic of motion. Inertia, he says, is like a friend that makes things want to keep moving. When Newton slides down the slide, inertia whispers, 'Keep going! I love rolling!' It's the force that wants objects to stay in motion, a playful energy that makes sliding down the slide a delightful adventure.

FRICTION

Now, let's talk about friction – our orchard's gentle stopper. When the slide fun ends, friction steps in, saying, 'Take a little break, Apple.' Friction is like a friendly force that slows things down, the one that gently stops Newton's rolling. It's the reason the slide's excitement can't last forever, offering a cozy pause after the playful dance with inertia. Together, inertia and friction create a harmonious balance on the slide.

LEVERAGE

Take a ride on the seesaw, and you'll discover the power of leverage. Leverage is like a teamwork trick that makes lifting someone on the other end feel easier.
When you sit closer to the center (the fulcrum) of the seesaw, it's a balancing act. But, if a friend sits farther away, it's like having a lever superhero. Even if your friend is heavier, you can still lift them up!

FULCRUM

Newton shows his apple pals that leverage is all about finding the perfect balance. Move closer or farther from the fulcrum, and you'll experience the seesaw's physics dance. It's the seesaw secret that turns every up-and-down into a playful physics lesson in our orchard playground!

CENTRIPETAL FORCE

Newton, our orchard scientist, uncovered the mesmerizing force at play on the merry-go-round – it's called centripetal force! When you hop on the merry-go-round and it starts spinning, the force that keeps you moving in a circle is centripetal force.

It's like a magical hand saying, "Stay close, little apple!" Centripetal force pulls everything toward the center of the spinning action. As you feel the whirl of the merry-go-round, you're experiencing the invisible force that keeps you on the ride.

CENTRIFUGAL FORCE

But, here's the fascinating part – when you step off the merry-go-round, you feel a force trying to push you away. It's the opposite force called centrifugal force, trying to send you on a straight path. Newton loves to demonstrate this merry-go-round marvel, showing how centripetal force keeps things spinning and centrifugal force comes into play when you step away.

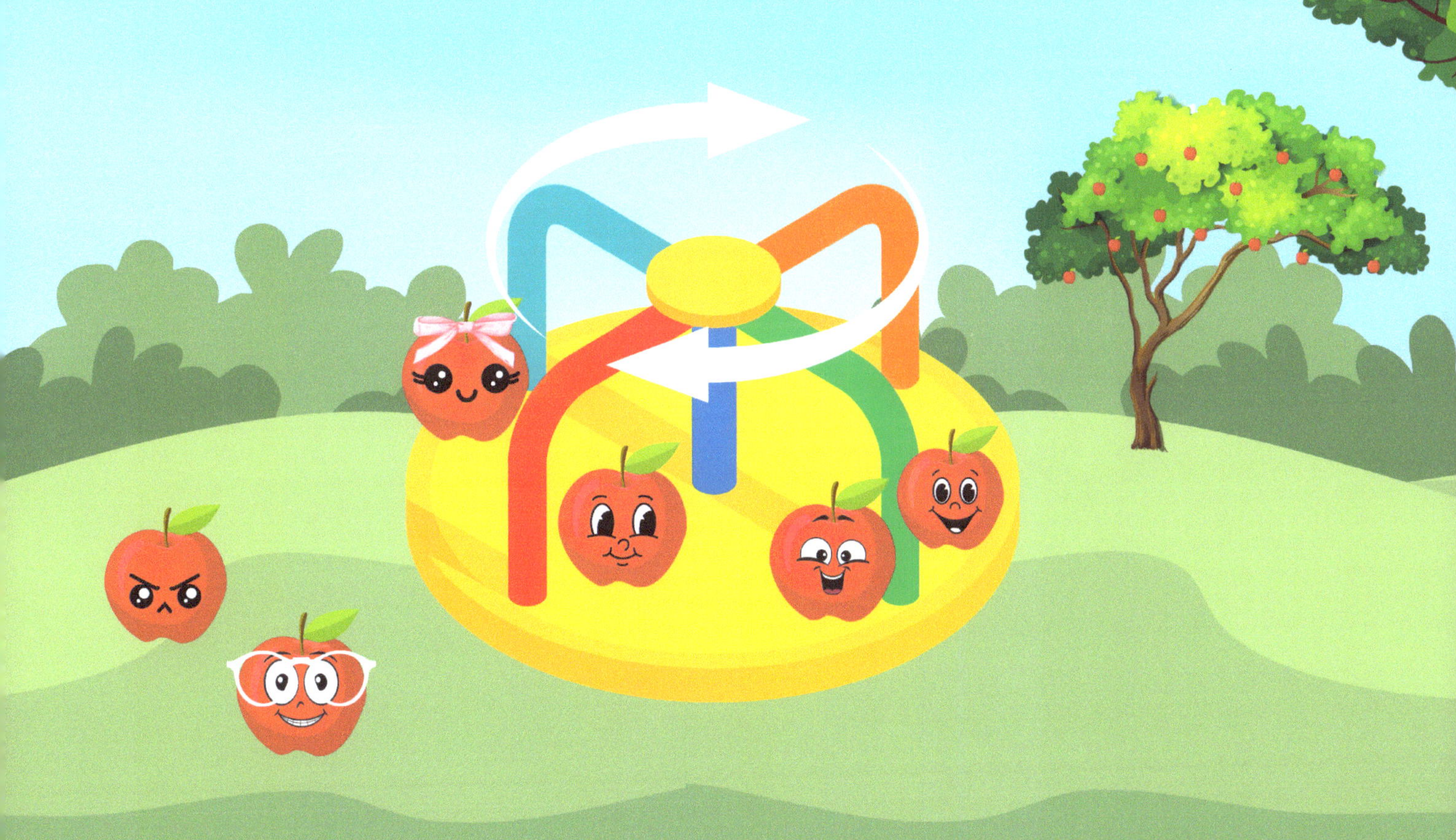

COMPRESSION

Newton, our bouncy guide, is ready to unveil the hidden energy magic on the spring rider! When you sit on the spring rider, you might notice a little squish - that's compression at work. But, here's the cool part: as the spring compresses, it's storing energy, like a springy battery getting charged.

That stored energy is potential energy, waiting for the perfect moment to turn into motion. When you release the spring, it unleashes that stored energy, propelling you back up in a delightful bounce. It's like the spring saying, "I've got energy to spare - let's bounce and play!"

POTENTIAL ENERGY

So, every time you bounce on the spring rider, you're tapping into the spring's stored potential energy, turning each compression into a joyful burst of motion. Newton encourages his apple pals to feel the squish, understand the stored energy, and bounce away with the playful physics of the spring rider in our orchard playground!

BUOYANCY

Newton, our buoyancy explorer, invites you to discover the floating wonders of the orchard pond! When apples take a dip in the water, they experience a force called **buoyancy.**

Buoyancy is like an invisible hand lifting the apples, saying, "Stay afloat, little friends!" Newton explains that objects float or sink based on their weight and the water's pushback. If an apple is lighter than the water it displaces, it floats happily on the surface.

In the quiet orchard night, Newton shares the moon's special dance. "Look at the moon! It's like a big ballerina doing a dance called 'orbit.' Orbit is a fancy word for going in a big circle. The moon's dance is with Earth – they're space buddies who can't resist each other's pull. Gravity is what keeps them close, like a hug in space. So, every night, the moon twirls around Earth in its beautiful orbit dance, making sure it never falls down. Sleep tight, and dream of the moon's dance in the sky!

ORBIT

DRAW YOURSELF AS AN APPLE!

CIRCLE TWO TYPES OF ENERGY YOU HAVE LEARNED ABOUT!

I hope you had as much fun exploring the physics playground as I did showing you around! If my adventures with forces, motion, and gravity made your day brighter and your brain spark with curiosity, I have a small favor to ask. **Could you hop onto Amazon and leave a review for 'Newton's Playground Physics' by Lady Appleton?** Your thoughts mean a whole universe to us and help other young scientists join in on the fun. Don't forget – every star counts in our galaxy of learning! Thanks a bunch (of apples)!"

www.ingramcontent.com/pod-product-compliance
Lightning Source LLC
LaVergne TN
LVHW071227160826
845679LV00003B/925